really easy piano

CLASSICAL

ISBN: 978-1-84449-568-9

Visit Hal Leonard Online at
www.halleonard.com

World headquarters, contact:
Hal Leonard
7777 West Bluemound Road
Milwaukee, WI 53213
Email: info@halleonard.com

In Europe, contact:
Hal Leonard Europe Limited
1 Red Place
London, W1K 6PL
Email: info@halleonardeurope.com

In Australia, contact:
Hal Leonard Australia Pty. Ltd.
4 Lentara Court
Cheltenham, Victoria, 3192 Australia
Email: info@halleonard.com.au

really easy piano

Autumn
(from 'The Four Seasons')

Music by Antonio Vivaldi

Antonio Vivaldi was born and raised in Venice. He became known as the Red Priest after taking holy orders because of his red hair. From 1703 to 1740 he worked for the Ospedale della Pieta which was a school for orphan girls. He trained them and composed operas, cantatas, and chamber music for the girls to perform. However, it is the 450 or so concertos that have made Vivaldi famous in the recent past. Of these, certainly the most famous are the four that comprise *The Four Seasons*, perhaps because of the vividly descriptive sonnets that Vivaldi attached to each concerto.

Hints & Tips: Keep this piece very 'rigid' and the dotted rhythms accurate.

Can-Can
(from 'Orpheus In The Underworld')

Music by Jacques Offenbach

Offenbach was chiefly remembered along with Johann Strauss II as the pre-eminent composer of popular music during the 19th century. The Can-Can is taken from a two-act operetta entitled *Orpheus In The Underworld* composed in 1858. Offenbach first gained recognition as a virtuoso cellist and wrote several works for the instrument, including the 'Concerto Militaire' and the 'Concertino'. He then became a conductor and rented a theatre in which he could stage his light-hearted operettas.

Hints & Tips: This well-known piece should be played lightly and fairly quickly. Pay attention to all of the articualation marks, i.e. staccato, accents and tenuto.

The Blue Danube

Music by Johann Strauss II

Johann Strauss II came from a very musical family. His father was a composer, and tried to stop his son from taking up music as a profession. When this failed, the younger Strauss employed his two younger brothers to help rehearse his concert band when he needed time to compose. 'The Blue Danube' remains his most popular work, along with the operetta, *Die Fledermaus*. Brahms was great friends with the younger Strauss, and remarked to him once how much he would have liked to have written 'The Blue Danube' theme.

Hints & Tips: Keep the second and third beats in the left hand very light.

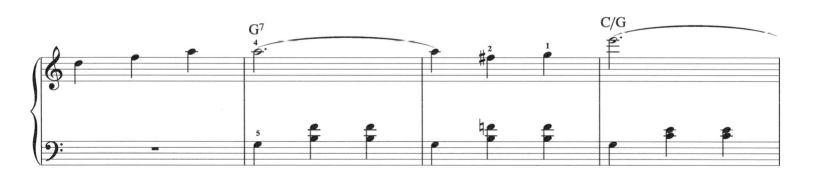

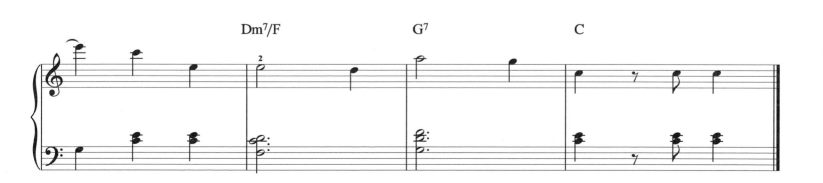

Clair de Lune

(from 'Suite Bergamasque')

Music by Claude Debussy

Debussy composed his *Suite Masques et Bergamasques*, in which 'Clair de Lune' appears, around 1890. However, it was only revised and published in 1905. He is without doubt one of the originators of modernism in western music influencing many younger composers including Stravinsky, Messiaen and Varèse. The label 'impressionist' has haunted Debussy's reputation. This may be because Debussy preferred to find inspiration in paintings. He told Edgard Varèse in 1911 "I love paintings almost as much as I love music".

Hints & Tips: Look at the time signature. It means that there are nine quavers (eighth notes) in each bar, grouped as three dotted crotchet (quarter note) beats.

Clarinet Concerto

(Theme)

Music by Wolfgang Amadeus Mozart

This was the last concerto of any kind that Mozart wrote. It was interestingly written for the bassett clarinet; a rare instrument nowadays, with a lower register than the modern instrument. Mozart responded to the fine playing of Anton Stadler in writing this piece, for whom he had already composed the clarinet quintet.

Hints & Tips: Make sure you fully practise the right hand and left hand 'question/answer' passage (bars 9-12) so one runs on smoothly from the other.

Dance Of The Sugar Plum Fairy

(from 'The Nutcracker')

Music by Pyotr Ilyich Tchaikovsky

This is from *The Nutcracker*, first performed in 1892. It is a fantasy tale about a young girl, Clara, who becomes infatuated with a toy nutcracker. At midnight all her toys come to life to ward off an attack from an army of mice. The toy nutcracker then turns into a Prince and both Clara and the Prince travel to the land of the Sugar Plum Fairy. Tchaikovsky's death a year later remains the subject of debate. He is reputed to have drunk some un-boiled water from which he contracted cholera.

Hints & Tips: This piece was written for celesta, a keyboard instrument which sounds like little bells. Try playing the right hand an octave higher to imitate this sound.

Eine Kleine Nachtmusik

Music by Wolfgang Amadeus Mozart

Composed in August 1787, in Vienna, this serenade was conceived around two years after the series of six quartets dedicated to Haydn that marked Mozart's mature style in this form. Haydn once confessed to Mozart's father that "before God and as an honest man I tell you that your son is the greatest composer known to me either in person or by name". At the time Mozart was writing *Eine Kleine Nachtmusik*, he was already preoccupied with Don Giovanni as well as finding time to compose some of the finest string quintets ever written.

Hints & Tips: Make sure the notes in the first four bars sound exactly together.
It may also be a good idea to practise bars 9 and 10 more thoroughly to get the semiquaver passages even.

Flow My Tears

Music by John Dowland

Dowland is recognised as the greatest English composer of lute music. He was born in 1563 in London but found more fame abroad than at home, probably because of his Catholicism which put him out of favour at Court. 'Flow My Tears' melancholic aspect was very appealing to Dowland's generation; indeed he made a pun on his name to highlight it: Dowland, semper dolens (Dowland, always grieving).

Hints & Tips: Keep a steady pulse and make your playing as smooth as possible.
Notice that the note C is sometimes sharp and sometimes natural.

The Happy Farmer

Music by Robert Schumann

This piece is one of the miniatures from *Album For The Young*. This set of children's piano pieces was composed in 1848 and became one of Schumann's best selling works. Schumann was as well known as a journalist and critic as he was a composer. He recognised the immense talent of both Chopin and the young Brahms and declared as much in his published articles. Schumann once tried to improve his piano technique by attaching wooden boards to his fingers; in doing so he permanently damaged his hands.

Hints & Tips: The left hand has the tune for most of the time.
Keep the right hand quavers (eighth notes) very light.

Fantasie Impromptu

Music by Frédéric Chopin

Written in 1835, the 'Fantasie Impromptu' gave Chopin great trouble during its composition and he was never happy with it. Consequently it was only published posthumously along with six or seven other unfinished works despite the fact that he had expressly asked for these pieces to be destroyed after his death. Chopin's other chief works are characterised by technical brilliance and virtuosity but always at the service of a graceful poetic instinct.

Hints & Tips: Play this beautiful piece with feeling and try to sense where it should get louder and softer. Practise the semiquaver turns in bars 22 and 29 to get them even.

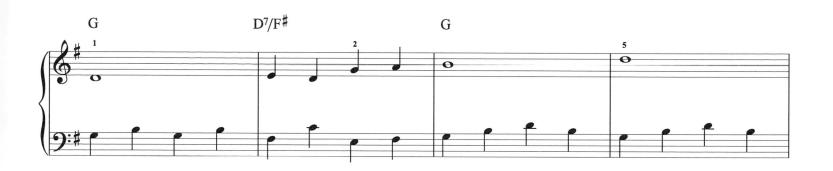

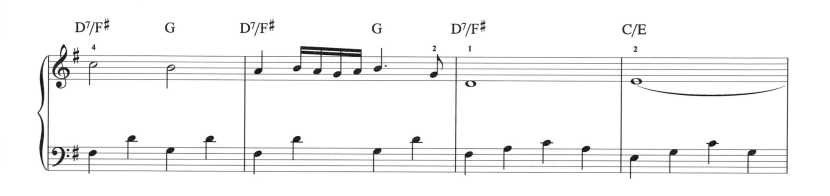

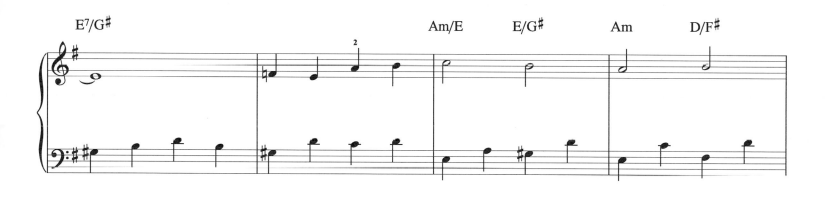

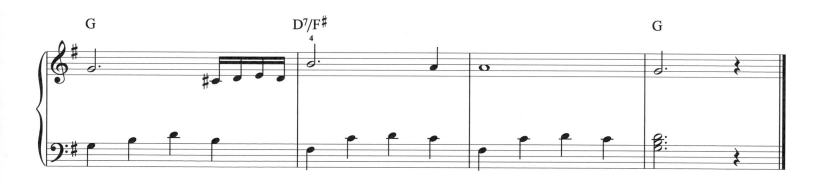

The Harmonious Blacksmith

Music by George Frideric Handel

'The Harmonious Blacksmith' was the nickname for the 'Air and Variations' from Handel's *5th Harpsichord Suite*, written around 1720. Nobody really knows how the piece got its name. Some sources say that Handel was sheltering from the rain when he heard a blacksmith singing the tune, but that is almost certainly fictitious. Handel was supported by his patron George, the Elector of Hanover, who later became George I of England and it was for him that Handel composed his celebrated *Water Music* performed on a barge sailing on the Thames.

Hints & Tips: Take care with the fingering and keep a good steady beat.

La Ci Darem La Mano

(from 'Don Giovanni')

Music by Wolfgang Amadeus Mozart

This duet from *Don Giovanni*, composed in 1787, concerns Zerlina, a peasant girl already betrothed to Masetto, and the attempts of the Don to seduce her. The baritone, Luigi Bassi, who created the title-role, was upset that he had no big aria to show off his skills as a singer and complained to Mozart. It is said that Mozart re-composed 'La Ci Darem La Mano' five times before Bassi said he was happy with it.

Hints & Tips: Play this piece lightly and watch out out for the slurs.

La Donna E Mobile

(from 'Rigoletto')

Music by Giuseppe Verdi

This is the famous tenor aria from Verdi's opera *Rigoletto*, first performed in Venice, March 1851. Verdi knew that the tune would be a sure-fire hit and so delayed giving the music to the leading tenor until the day of the opening, in order to preserve its impact. He was always furious about the common practice of famous singers inserting additional unwritten high notes into his music. However, that hasn't stopped it continuing even today!

Hints & Tips: Keep the left hand very light in this famous tenor aria.

Largo
(from 'From The New World' Symphony)

Music by Antonin Dvořák

Dvořák is a composer whose music often shows influences of the Czech folk music of his heritage. He moved to America for three years to become Director of the National Conservatory in New York. However, he was allowed almost four months holiday from this post which gave him time to compose. While holidaying he would most often go to the Czech community in Spillville, Iowa. It was this that gave him the inspiration to complete his best loved work, Symphony *From The New World*, premiered on December 16, 1897 in New York City.

Hints & Tips: Try to hold onto the left hand notes for their full length.
Your right hand needs to be very legato (smooth).

Marche Militaire

Music by Franz Schubert

The three military marches that make up a larger work date from the summer of 1818 when Schubert was 21 years old. The works were written originally for piano duet, a form which in Schubert composed a number of works. The man who dominated musical life in Vienna and influenced Schubert more than any other was Beethoven. However, Beethoven's temper was so stormy and unpredictable that Schubert never plucked up the courage to speak to him. The older composer, when given some of Schubert's compositions on his deathbed, was delighted and recognised the "divine spark" of Schubert's genius.

Hints & Tips: If you can't manage the repeated semiquavers (sixteenth notes) in the left hand to start with, omit the second of each pair.

Minuet
(from 'String Quintet No.5')

Music by Luigi Boccherini

Born in Lucca in 1743, Boccherini showed his talent early. By the time he was 14 he had travelled to Vienna to play the cello where he quickly established his name as a virtuoso. He is now chiefly remembered for the Minuet from *String Quintet No.5*. However, he also wrote many cello concertos and also quintets for strings and guitar. Boccherini lived in appalling poverty after the death of his Spanish benefactor, his misery further heightened by the death of his two sons. His death passed virtually unnoticed by the musical fraternity.

Hints & Tips: The most tricky parts of this piece are the octave jumps, e.g. bars 1 and 3.
Practise getting to the lower note quickly.

Morning
(from 'Peer Gynt')
Music by Edvard Grieg

Grieg studied at the Leipzig conservatoire and was already famous, having completed his piano concerto in 1868. He tried unsuccessfully to collaborate with others to create an opera, however, he did create a series of incidental pieces for Henrik Ibsen's play *Peer Gynt*, which dates from 1875 and this is the most famous of them. Although in later life he became chronically ill, he continued to compose and give concerts until his death in 1907.

Hints & Tips: Look out for the accidentals in the right hand from bar 8 onwards.
Remember an accidental lasts right through the bar.

O For The Wings Of A Dove

Music by Felix Mendelssohn

Mendelssohn was very well received in England and this song is from the hymn *Hear My Prayer* written specially for English performance, and which became very popular during the Victorian era. First performed in January 1845, the piece is scored for organ, chorus and boy soprano soloist. While in England Mendelssohn was received by Queen Victoria and she commented to her diary that he was:
"such an agreeable, clever man and his countenance beams with intelligence and genius."

Hints & Tips: Take care that the notes in the left hand chords sound exactly together. The last four bars in the right hand also need special practice.

Minuet In G

(from 'Anna Magdelena Notebook')

Music by Johann Sebastian Bach

Bach came to work for Prince Leopold in Köthen, in 1717, lured by the large orchestra which the Prince kept, and of course a large sum of money. There he wrote some of his finest chamber music including the *Brandenburg Concertos*. Unfortunately, whilst here, Bach's first wife was taken ill and died. This minuet is taken from the two books of collected pieces that Bach compiled for his second wife Anna Magdalena. She was the daughter of one of the musicians in the orchestra and apparently a gifted soprano. She was some 16 years younger than Bach.

Hints & Tips: Watch out for bars such as bar 7 where the left hand plays staccato and the right hand plays smoothly. This technique will take a bit more practice.

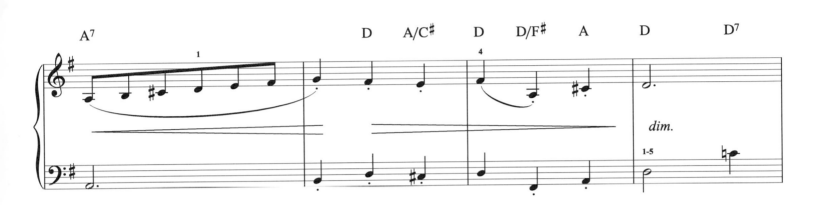

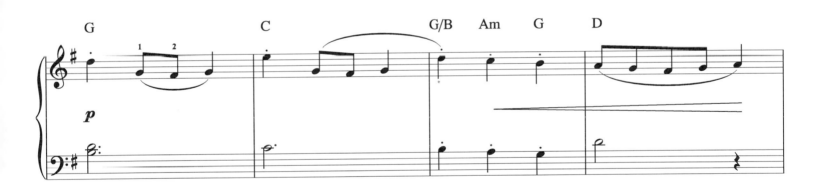

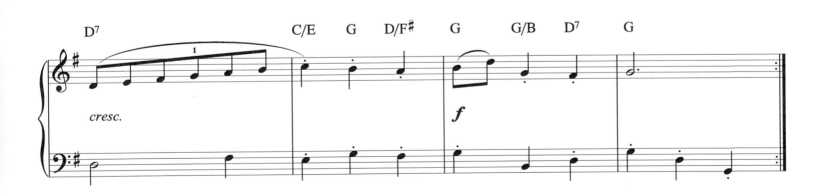

Ode To Joy
(from 'Symphony No.9')

Music by Ludwig van Beethoven

This is the main theme from the last movement of Beethoven's final symphony, the ninth. However it took six years to complete, being written between 1817 and 1823. The premiere was given on May 7, 1824 in Vienna by which time the composer was completely deaf. He could not conduct but still stood on the platform next to the conductor to indicate the tempo. When the work was over, Beethoven failed to turn around to acknowledge the rapturous applause, and it took one of the soloists to turn him round to see that the piece was a success.

Hints & Tips: This theme from the 'Choral' Symphony is best known to many as the EEC anthem. It needs to be played with spirit.

Pavane

Music by Gabriel Fauré

Written in 1887, the 'Pavane' is one of Fauré's best works, although at the time the composer did not think so.
Fauré had been doing a great deal of travelling and he wrote a letter to a friend saying "the only thing I have
been able to compose in this shuttlecock existence is a Pavane – elegant, assuredly, but not particularly important".
Originally Fauré set a poem to the tune of the Pavane for a chorus to sing along with the orchestra.
However, nowadays the work is almost always performed without the additional chorus.

Hints & Tips: Keep the left hand crotchets (quarter notes) very steady,
and take care with the right hand rhythms.

Polovtsian Dance

(from 'Prince Igor')

Music by Alexander Borodin

Borodin always remained by profession a chemistry professor, but was a remarkably gifted amateur composer. The Polovtsian Dances, from the opera *Prince Igor* composed in 1875, remain the most popular of his works, chiefly because he used one of the themes from the song, 'A Stranger In Paradise'. Unfortunately, the opera was far from complete at the time of Borodin's death and it took both Rimsky-Korsakov and Glazunov to assemble a score and to fill in the missing details including over 1,000 bars of music in Act III. It was finally given its premiere on October 23, 1894.

Hints & Tips: Practise hands separately until you are sure of all the notes. Hold the left hand chords their full value.

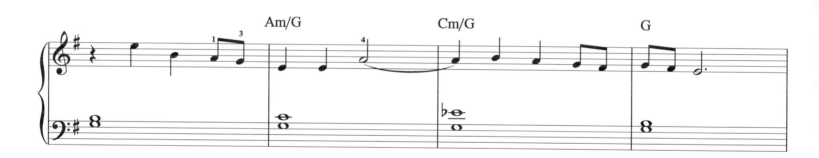

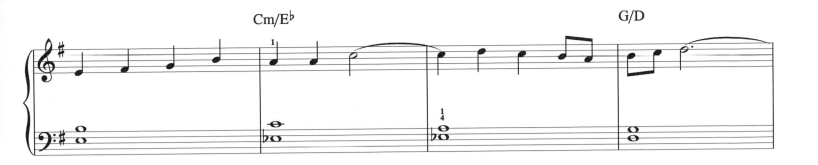

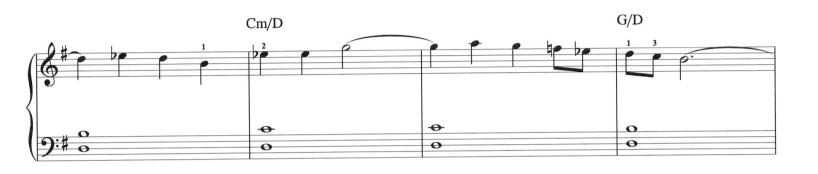

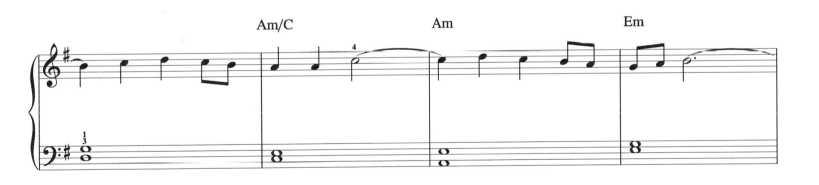

Prelude No.1

Music by Johann Sebastian Bach

This is the first piece in book one of *The Well-Tempered Clavier* and was written during Bach's time in Köthen around 1722. The book contains a prelude and fugue in each of the 24 musical keys (12 major and 12 minor). The title does not refer to whether the keyboard is in a good mood, rather it refers to Bach's invention of the modern equal temperament tuning, which facilitates changing from one key to another easily. Bach sought to utilise this new tuning to compose in as many different keys as possible.

Hints & Tips: Be sure to hold the left hand notes right through the bar. The right hand should be as smooth and even as possible.

Sarabande In D Minor

Music by George Frideric Handel

As Handel was such an accomplished keyboard player, it is unsurprising that as a young man he wrote a great deal of fine pieces for the instrument. When in London, Handel published two large sets of keyboard suites, the first set of eight in 1720, and the second set of eight in 1733.
This stately Sarabande is taken from the 4th suite of the 2nd set.

Hints & Tips: The sarabande was a slow and stately dance.
Be aware of a steady three beats in each bar.

The Swan
(from 'The Carnival Of The Animals')

Music by Camille Saint-Saëns

'The Swan' was written for solo cello and is taken from Saint-Saëns perennially popular *The Carnival Of The Animals* which was premiered on March 9, 1886. The work as a whole shows off Saint-Saëns sense of humour and parodies music by amongst others, Offenbach, Rossini and Berlioz. He never allowed it to be published in its entirety during his lifetime, preferring to publish 'The Swan' on its own instead. Upon his death however instructions were found that it should be published complete. Saint-Saëns was continually disappointed at the work's popularity at the expense of his more serious work, and feared that it would be the only thing for which he would be remembered.

Hints & Tips: The right hand melody should be played smoothly and with expression.
Practise the left hand well, as it has to stretch quite far, sometimes over an octave.

The Skater's Waltz

Music by Emile Waldteufel

Waldteufel was born in Strasbourg in 1837 and studied at the Paris Conservatoire alongside Massenet.
He was appointed court pianist to Napoleon III in 1865. His renown was confined to France until he received an
introduction to the Prince of Wales (later Edward VII) and signed a long-term publishing contract with a London firm.
He wrote many waltzes, polkas, mazurkas and other dance pieces including, in 1882, 'The Skater's Waltz'.
Waldteufel is now remembered as the finest composer of waltzes after the Strauss family.

Hints & Tips: The right hand needs to be smooth and sustained,
while the left hand notes should be light and rather detached.

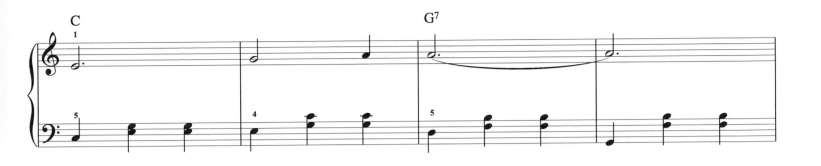

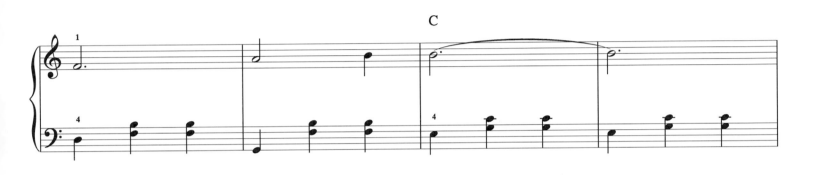

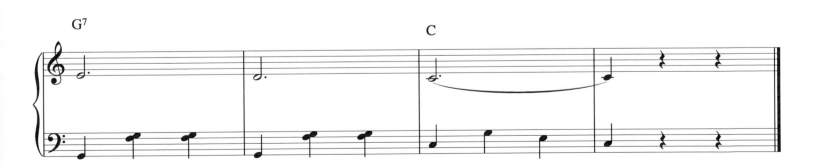

Symphony No.40
(Theme)

Music by Wolfgang Amadeus Mozart

This is the 2nd of the final triptych of symphonies that Mozart composed.
Astonishingly, all three symphonies were composed in less than three months in the summer of 1788.
Symphony No.40 was probably performed in May 1789. It seems incredible today, but apparently the
concert was poorly attended and Mozart being the spend thrift he was gave half of the tickets away.

Hints & Tips: This piece needs to be taken quite quickly.
Try to keep the tempo (speed) steady throughout.

'Surprise' Symphony
(Theme)

Music by Joseph Haydn

This is the second of the *London Symphonies* composed in 1791 and premiered on March 23, 1792. Haydn was very warmly received in London and he commented that he "could dine out every night" given the amount of invitations he received. The loud 'surprise' chord in the Andante section was inserted because a former pupil, Pleyel, had also travelled to London to set up a rival series of concerts. Haydn said he wanted "to surprise the public with something new and to début in a brilliant manner in order to prevent my rank from being usurped by my pupil Pleyel".

Hints & Tips: Practise the right hand very slowly with the correct fingering.
The swapping of fingers is a good technique to learn because it helps keep the notes very light and even.

Theme From Swan Lake

Music by Pyotr Ilyich Tchaikovsky

This is from the ballet of the same name which premiered on January 15, 1895. When first performed, the piece was subject to vicious cuts and re-ordering of the music, probably because of Tchaikovsky's attitude to collaboration which meant he was not interested in the proposed staging at all. The mutilation of the work forced him to change his attitude and communicate more effectively with dramatists and choreographers.

Hints & Tips: Make sure all of of the notes in the left hand chords sound together when you play. This piece is meant to be played *legato* (smoothly) all the way through.

To A Wild Rose

Music by Edward MacDowell

'To A Wild Rose' is the first of MacDowell's *Woodland Sketches*, a suite of piano pieces dating from 1896. The pieces in *Woodland Sketches* evoke pastoral scenes from the American countryside. MacDowell, though born in New York, learnt piano and composition in Paris and also at various cities in Germany. He was talented enough to play in concerts for Liszt at the Frankfurt Conservatoire and this certainly furthered his career.

Hints & Tips: Watch out for the fingering in this one – the swapping of fingers makes the notes even and emphasises the slurs.

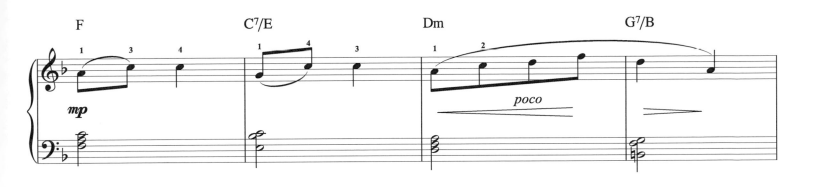

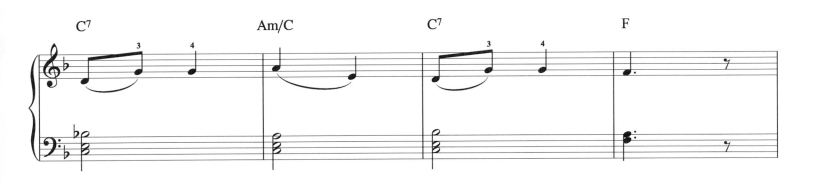

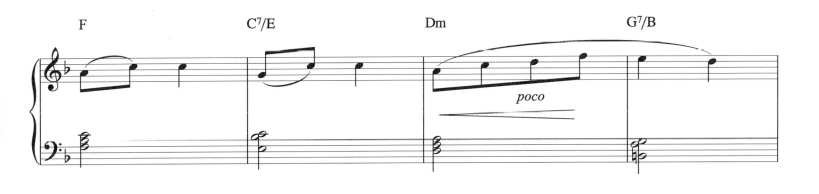

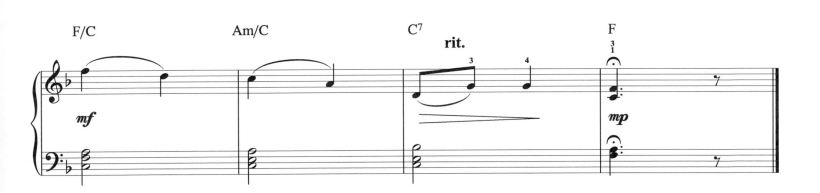

Toreador's Song
(from 'Carmen')

Music by Georges Bizet

This is the song the toreador Escamillo uses to impress Carmen, taken from Bizet's most famous work. The opera *Carmen*, when premiered in 1875, met with terrible reviews, and the already ill Bizet died shortly thereafter, never tasting the success the opera achieves today. Bizet's other operas faired little better in terms of reviews. The librettists of the opera *The Pearl Fishers* declared, when they heard what spectacular music had been written, that they would have tried harder with the drama if they had known what a fine composer Bizet was.

Hints & Tips: Take care to make a real difference between the dotted quaver/semiquaver groups and the even quavers which occur from bar 10 onwards.

Trout Quintet
(4th Movement Theme)

Music by Franz Schubert

The piano quintet 'The Trout' was written in the summer of 1819. Schubert was inspired during a holiday visit to the Austrian mountains and whilst there wrote one of his most enduring pieces of chamber music. Rather than the conventional scoring, Schubert replaced one of the violins with a double bass, to allow the cello to have a more melodic role. The name of the work comes from the title of one of Schubert's songs, the theme of which is used in the 4th movement featured here.

Hints & Tips: The tune (top notes in the right hand) needs to be heard clearly.

Trumpet Voluntary

Music by Jeremiah Clarke

Composer and organist Jeremiah Clarke was born in London 1674. 'Trumpet Voluntary' is the more widely used title for 'The Prince Of Denmark's March' which occurs in his publication *Choice Lessons For The Harpsichord And Spinet*. He supposedly shot himself in 1707 because of an unhappy love affair.

Hints & Tips: Imitating the sound and style of trumpet music, this piece needs to be played rather like a march.

Waltz

Music by Johannes Brahms

Having edited some of Schubert's waltzes for four hands in 1864, the young Brahms decided to create his own collection of waltzes for piano duet. These were completed around January 1865. Throughout his life, Brahms felt inferior as a composer, particularly in respect of Beethoven. This led him to be harshly self-critical, and he often burned music he was less than happy with. Apparently, as many as 20 string quartets were burned before he published his first.

Hints & Tips: Practise the right hand alone first. Then try to feel a single pulse in each bar rather than three.

Wedding March
(from 'A Midsummer Night's Dream')

Music by Felix Mendelssohn

Mendelssohn was indisputably the most talented child prodigy after Mozart in the history of western music. He was composing fluently by the age of 12 as well as excelling in languages, poetry and literature. He was just 17 when the incidental music to *A Midsummer Night's Dream* was written. The last of the pieces in this suite is the now familiar 'Wedding March'. He was also responsible for reviving and re-invigorating the oratorio with his own works, *Elijah* and *St Paul*.

Hints & Tips: The groups of three quavers (eighth notes) are called triplets. They should be played evenly, each note lasting a third of a crotchet (quarter note) beat.

William Tell Overture

(from 'William Tell')

Music by Gioacchino Rossini

William Tell is the last opera that Rossini wrote before his early retirement at the age of only 37. It was premiered in Paris on August 3, 1829. The lead tenor part is almost supernaturally difficult and extremely long (the opera, given complete would last some five hours). Although revived sporadically, the overture is almost certainly the most popular piece Rossini ever wrote, and has become world famous. Rossini, who loved fine food as much as he loved music, is responsible for the creation of the recipe 'Tournedos a la Rossini'.

Hints & Tips: Be sure to put your thumb on the fourth notes in the right hand of bars 6 and 14.

Discover our range of really easy piano bumper books...

ORDER NO. AM995643   ORDER NO. AM1000615   ORDER NO. AM999449   ORDER NO. AM997744

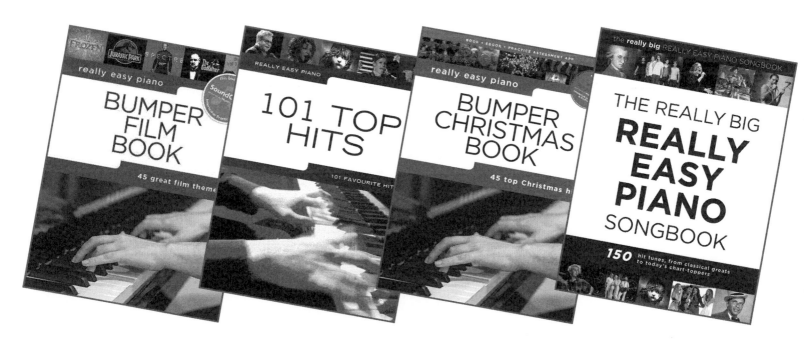

ORDER NO. HLE90004915   ORDER NO. AM1008975   ORDER NO. AM1013331   ORDER NO. AM1011032

Just visit your local music shop and ask
to see our huge range of music in print.